Original title:
Where Emotions Grow

Copyright © 2024 Creative Arts Management OÜ
All rights reserved.

Author: William Hawthorne
ISBN HARDBACK: 978-9916-88-828-5
ISBN PAPERBACK: 978-9916-88-829-2

Leaves of Reflection

Rustling whispers on the breeze,
Golden hues where sunlight weaves.
Every leaf a story tells,
In quiet corners, nature dwells.

Shadows dance upon the ground,
In their grace, lost dreams are found.
Fleeting moments, rich and bright,
Captured softly in the light.

Each day fades to twilight's glow,
Underneath, the rivers flow.
Time unfurls its gentle map,
In the hush, the heart finds lap.

Echoes linger, sweet and clear,
Whispers of all we hold dear.
As seasons change and old gives birth,
In leaves of gold, we find our worth.

The Touch of Tomorrow

Beneath the dawn's embrace we rise,
With hopes that stretch across the skies.
Every moment, bold and new,
The world awakens, kissed with dew.

Paths of futures, unworn, divine,
Step by step, our dreams align.
In the heartbeat of today,
Lies the promise of the way.

Waves of change, with subtle grace,
Guide us through this sacred space.
With every breath, we build and grow,
In the light of what we sow.

Whispers tell of love and fight,
In shadows cast by morning light.
Together finding strength and grace,
In the touch of tomorrow's face.

Petals of Yesterday's Hopes

Petals fall on silent ground,
Whispers of the dreams we've found.
Colors fade in evening light,
Hopes bloom softly, drifting slight.

The Blooming of Silent Echoes

In shadows where the silence grows,
Echoes dance where no one goes.
Floral scents in twilight air,
Nature breathes a timeless prayer.

Fields of Fragile Joy

In fields where laughter used to play,
Fragile blossoms greet the day.
Each petal holds a memory,
Of fleeting moments, wild and free.

Echoes of Elysian Heights

Above the clouds, the whispers soar,
Echoes drift to every shore.
In the heights where dreams collide,
Life unfolds, a gentle tide.

Fragments of Passion

In whispers soft, hearts intertwine,
Shadows dance, where stars align.
Each glance a spark, ignites the night,
Fragments of love, pure and bright.

Boundless dreams, like waves they roll,
Tender touches, a warm console.
In every sigh, a story spun,
Fragments of us, forever one.

The Bridge of Bonds

Across the river, hearts must meet,
With every step, our souls repeat.
A bridge of trust, both wide and strong,
Where laughter echoes, a joyful song.

As seasons change and time flows on,
This bond we share, a timeless dawn.
Hand in hand, we'll face the tide,
On this bridge, our hopes abide.

Silent Symphonies

In quiet moments, music breathes,
A symphony that gently weaves.
Notes like whispers, sweet and low,
Silent melodies, hearts in tow.

The moonlight plays on empty streets,
Where shadows dance, and silence greets.
In unseen chords, our souls are found,
Silent symphonies, profound sound.

The Veil of Sentiment

A fragile veil, so softly draped,
Hides all the words, the heart has craped.
Behind the layers, emotions swirl,
In the quiet, our secrets twirl.

With every sigh, the fabric sways,
Revealing truths in hidden ways.
This veil of sentiment, worn with grace,
Holds the essence of our embrace.

Roots of the Heart

In the quiet ground they lay,
Hidden dreams beneath the clay.
Nurtured by the rain's soft sigh,
Reaching out as time goes by.

Tangled up in silent grace,
Whispers of a sacred place.
All the love we've ever known,
Stands together, deeply grown.

Gardens of the Soul

In the morning light they bloom,
Colors chase away the gloom.
Petals dance with gentle ease,
Swaying softly in the breeze.

Every scent a story tells,
Magic from our secret wells.
In this garden, hearts unfold,
Each flower bright, each tale bold.

Whispers of the Heartstrings

Softly plays the secret tune,
Underneath the silver moon.
Notes that flutter, rise and fall,
Echo in the silent hall.

Every beat a story spun,
Rhythms that unite as one.
Strings entwined in life's embrace,
Whispers linger in this space.

The Orchard of Feelings

Beneath the boughs of tender care,
Fruits of joy hang rich and rare.
With each harvest, love transcends,
In this orchard where all bends.

Roots run deep in shared delight,
Harvesting by day and night.
Every bite a memory sweet,
In this orchard, hearts complete.

Tides of Sentiment

Waves crash softly on the shore,
Whispers of love forever more.
Gentle pulls, a rhythmic dance,
Hearts entwined in a timeless trance.

Moonlit nights, the silver gleam,
Carrying wishes, sweet as cream.
In the silence, soft and deep,
Tides of sentiment, secrets keep.

The Echoes of Feeling

In the chambers of the heart,
Every love begins as art.
Brushstrokes of joy, shades of pain,
Echoes linger like a sweet refrain.

Moments fleeting, voices blend,
Soft reminders that never end.
Songs of laughter, whispers low,
The echoes of feeling, softly flow.

Blossoms of the Soul

Petals unfurl in the warm embrace,
Each bloom a memory, a sacred space.
Tender scents dance in the air,
Blossoms of the soul, beyond compare.

Colors vibrant, stories told,
In every flower, love unfolds.
Seasons change, yet roots remain,
Nurtured by joy, watered by pain.

Roots in the Rain

Drizzle kisses the thirsty ground,
Nature's whisper, a soothing sound.
With each drop, the earth awakes,
Roots in the rain, the heart it takes.

Clouds bear witness to our dreams,
Binding us tightly in silent schemes.
Through storms, we grow, together strong,
Finding strength where we belong.

Stirrings of the Spirit

In the quiet dawn's embrace,
Whispers of hope take their flight,
Echoes of dreams softly trace,
Awakening hearts with delight.

In the shimmer of morning light,
Gentle shadows start to sway,
Unseen forces take to height,
Guiding the soul's tender way.

As the wildflowers bloom free,
Colors dance on the soft breeze,
Spirit's song, a sweet decree,
Inviting peace, a gentle tease.

With each pulse, the heart ignites,
Reminding us of our worth,
In the moonlit starry nights,
Stirrings of magic and mirth.

Paths of Introspection

Down the winding roads I tread,
Where thoughts like rivers freely flow,
Each step, a journey to be led,
In the depths, my spirit grows.

Shadows dance as silence reigns,
Echoing whispers in the mind,
Lost in layers of joy and pains,
A tapestry of life entwined.

Through the mirror of the soul,
Reflections flicker, truth revealed,
Finding pieces to feel whole,
In the darkness, light's concealed.

As I wander through my heart,
Braving shadows, facing fears,
With each moment, I impart,
Wisdom gained through countless years.

The Dance of Desire

In the hush of twilight's glow,
Hearts beat fast, a thrilling chase,
With each glance, the embers grow,
Lost in longing's warm embrace.

Spinning dreams on summer nights,
Under stars, two souls collide,
In the rhythm, pure delights,
This is where the magic hides.

Touch ignites a fierce desire,
Softly whispered wishes shared,
Every kiss, a burning fire,
In passion's depths, we are bared.

With each heartbeat, we entwine,
In the dance, the world fades out,
Bound by love, our hearts align,
In this moment, there's no doubt.

Cradled in Calm

In the silence, peace is found,
Gentle waves lap on the shore,
Nature's voice, a soothing sound,
Filling hearts with love, and more.

Underneath the timeless trees,
Whispers of the wind reside,
Cradled by the softest breeze,
In this space, we can confide.

With each breath, we find our ground,
As the world around us stills,
In this haven, joy abounds,
Time stands still, and so it fills.

Cradled in calm, we take flight,
Leaving worries far behind,
In the depths of love's pure light,
Finding solace, heart aligned.

Sunbeams on the Faces of Feelings

Golden rays touch every cheek,
Whispers of joy, never bleak.
In warm embrace, emotions glow,
Dancing brightly, hearts in tow.

Laughter spills like morning light,
Chasing shadows out of sight.
Every smile a fleeting song,
In this warmth, we all belong.

The Vineyards of Vivid Reminiscence

In rows of dreams, we gently tread,
Memories ripe, words left unsaid.
Each grape a story, sweet and bold,
In twilight's grip, our past unfolds.

Harvest moon casts silver beams,
Nurturing our forgotten dreams.
With every sip, the past awakes,
In every drop, a memory shakes.

Wellsprings of Warmth

Deep within, where kindness flows,
A quiet place, where comfort grows.
Each heartbeat echoes, soft and clear,
In wellsprings deep, we hold what's dear.

A gentle touch, a soothing word,
In these moments, souls are stirred.
Cascades of love, unbound and true,
In every heart, a flame anew.

Echoed Lullabies of the Heart

In distant whispers, soft and low,
A melody wrapped in moonlit glow.
Each note a treasure, deeply shared,
In twilight's hush, our spirits bared.

Nestled close, the world fades away,
As gentle tunes, like breezes play.
The heart's refrain, a timeless song,
In echoed dreams, we all belong.

The Canopy of Unspoken Desires

Beneath the leaves of whispered dreams,
Hushed secrets drift in moonlit streams.
Each glance a story left untold,
In shadows deep, our hearts unfold.

Silent wishes float on air,
Cloaked in hope, we sense the dare.
Branches twist, a dance of fate,
With every sigh, we bide, we wait.

Nestled close, the yearning stays,
In tender twilight, longing plays.
A forest thick with silent cries,
Where passion waits, and silence lies.

Harvesting Smiles in the Sun

In fields aglow with golden light,
We gather joy, the world feels bright.
Each laughter's spark, a treasure found,
In vibrant hues, our hearts unbound.

Breezes hum a cheerful tune,
Dancing warmth beneath the noon.
We pluck the moments, sweet and rare,
While nature sings without a care.

With every smile, the day expands,
Hope blooms softly in our hands.
Together, basking in the glow,
Harvesting love, as soft winds blow.

The Wildflowers of Longing

In meadows rich, where colors weave,
Wildflowers bloom, and hearts believe.
Each petal holds a tale so bright,
In fragrant whispers, day and night.

Softly swaying, a gentle plea,
To touch the depths of what can be.
The winds carry secrets untamed,
In the wild, our souls are named.

As sunlight kisses fields of dreams,
We linger lost in summer's beams.
With every breeze, a heartbeat calls,
In wildflower patches, longing sprawls.

A Haven for Heartfelt Revelations

In corners tucked, where shadows meet,
Whispers linger, soft and sweet.
A sanctuary built on trust,
In quiet moments, love is a must.

The walls are lined with truths we share,
Each secret held with tender care.
In every glance, a world we find,
A haven rich, our hearts entwined.

Embraced by silence, secrets bloom,
In this soft space, we chase the gloom.
A refuge where our souls can soar,
Heartfelt revelations, forevermore.

The Light in the Gloom

In the depths of the night, a flicker does gleam,
A whisper of hope, like a soft, gentle dream.
Through shadows and fears, it flickers and plays,
Lighting the corners of our darkest days.

A beacon of warmth, amidst chilling despair,
It dances like fire, the heart's tender flare.
Each ray a reminder, we're never alone,
In the light of the gloom, love finds us a home.

With courage ignited, we rise from our falls,
The glow guiding footsteps, as destiny calls.
In life's tangled web, where darkness once reigned,\nThe light in the gloom is a love uncontained.

So cherish the moments, let the radiance bloom,
For even in silence, there's force in the room.
Together we'll shine, two souls intertwined,
In the light of the gloom, forever aligned.

The Embrace of Understanding

In a world often cold, where voices clash loud,
Two hearts find solace, wrapped safe in a shroud.
With whispers of kindness, they bridge every gap,
In the embrace of understanding, they gently unwrap.

I see you, you see me, in this tranquil dance,
Navigating life's labyrinth, taking a chance.
With patience as strength, they walk hand in hand,
Through valleys of doubt, on love's solid land.

Words are like rivers, they flow and they wind,
In the depths of each story, true hearts are entwined.
With empathy's touch, misunderstandings dissolve,
In the embrace of understanding, we steadily evolve.

Moments spent sharing, bring clarity bright,
In the warmth of connection, we banish the night.
Together we flourish, as knowledge takes root,
In the embrace of understanding, our hearts find their suit.

Chasing Shadows

In the twilight's glow, we dance with the night,
Chasing the shadows, forever out of sight.
With each fleeting moment, they slip through our grasp,
In the play of the light, we silently clasp.

Fingers stretched out, reaching far to the dark,
Threads woven deeply, leaving a mark.
In the game of reflections, we spiral and spin,
Chasing the shadows, where the dreams begin.

But shadows are lessons, they teach us to see,
The depth of our fears, the strength of our glee.
For in each silhouette, there lies a great tale,
Chasing the shadows, we learn not to pale.

So wander in twilight, let the night be our guide,
For where shadows linger, our spirits abide.
In the search for the light, we find what we lack,
Chasing the shadows, we learn to look back.

The Aroma of Affinity

In the gardens of life, where friendships are sown,
An aroma of affinity, so tenderly grown.
Each petal a story, each fragrance a bond,
In the scent of connection, our souls correspond.

With laughter like blossoms, and kindness like dew,
The warmth of compassion wraps close like a brew.
In moments of silence, the heart's language speaks,
The aroma of affinity, in connection, it peaks.

Seasoned with memories, sweet spices of trust,
In the hearth of our hearts, it's a must, it's a must.
With every embrace, the scents intertwine,
In the aroma of affinity, our spirits align.

So breathe in the love, let it fill up the air,
In the fragrance of friendship, there's magic to share.
For in this bouquet, we find all we need,
The aroma of affinity, our souls' gentle creed.

The Pulse of Connection

In the quiet hum of the night,
Hearts whisper soft and light.
Fingers brush, a fleeting spark,
Binding souls, igniting dark.

Laughter dances on the breeze,
An embrace, a gentle squeeze.
Eyes meet, a knowing glance,
In the rhythm, lost in chance.

Distance fades, time stands still,
In this moment, we find will.
Threads of fate, woven tight,
Together we ignite the night.

A pulse that beats, two as one,
In the silence, love is spun.
Each heartbeat a sacred vow,
In this instant, here, and now.

Salty Waves of Regret

The ocean sighs, a heavy weight,
Whispers of love that turned to fate.
Footprints washed away by time,
Memories linger, lost in rhyme.

Salty tears on sandy shores,
Echoes of love behind closed doors.
Waves crash down in crashing pain,
Each tide carries a hint of rain.

Distant horizons, dreams uncaught,
Lessons of love too dearly bought.
In the swell of the darkened sea,
Regret flows deep and endlessly.

Yet from the depths, hope will rise,
New dawns beckon 'neath the skies.
The heart, though bruised, knows its song,
In salty waves where we belong.

The Labyrinth of Love

In the maze of hidden hearts,
Twists and turns, where love imparts.
Each corner turned reveals a dream,
A puzzle binding, hope's sweet scheme.

Lost in shadows, secrets kept,
Promises made that we have stepped.
With every choice, a path unfolds,
The story of love gently told.

Through the thorns, we find the light,
Guided by stars in the night.
In the labyrinth, we may roam,
But love will always lead us home.

Trust the journey, fear the fall,
For in this maze, we'll have it all.
Hand in hand, we'll write our fate,
In the labyrinth, love won't wait.

Seeds of Sentimentality

Underneath the old oak tree,
Whispers float, just you and me.
Memories planted, roots run deep,
In the soil of promises we keep.

Laughter sprouts with every kiss,
Moments cherished, pure bliss.
In every season, love will grow,
Tending dreams we come to know.

Tears may fall like summer rain,
Nourishing each joy and pain.
From little seeds, great wonders bloom,
Filling our hearts, dispelling gloom.

As we harvest what we've sown,
In each heartbeat, love has grown.
Together, planting dreams anew,
In fields of sentiment, me and you.

Veins of Passion

In the depths where shadows dance,
Whispers stir, a fleeting glance.
Blood ignites with each new spark,
Fires burn within the dark.

Echoes of a lover's sigh,
Like the wind that sweeps on by.
Heartbeat quickens, pulses race,
Love ignites in soft embrace.

Chasing dreams that feel so near,
Every touch, a reason here.
Veins alive with warmth and grace,
In this tender, timeless space.

Through the storm, our spirits soar,
Bound together, we want more.
In the depths of passion's flow,
Endless love we dare to show.

Threads of the Heart

Woven tight with golden strands,
Building bridges hand in hand.
Softly stitched with hopes anew,
Every thread in vibrant hue.

Beneath the weight of life's demand,
We find solace, understand.
Silent promises entwined,
In the fabric of our minds.

Each emotion, strong and bright,
Guides us through the darkest night.
With every knot, love's embrace,
We create our sacred space.

In the tapestry we weave,
Moments linger, hearts believe.
Threads connect, defining art,
Stitched together, soul and heart.

A Tapestry of Thoughts

Colors splash across the page,
Each idea, a silent stage.
Whispers of the mind unwind,
Frames of dreams we seek to find.

Sewing patterns, stitching light,
Words take shape, igniting night.
Every vision, bold and clear,
Crafts a story we hold dear.

In a world of endless seams,
Woven pathways lead to dreams.
Each chance taken, ink and breath,
Life's canvas dances, defies death.

Tapestries of love and pain,
In the depths, we find our gain.
Art of living, hearts combine,
Thoughts entwined, our fate aligns.

Sounds of Silence

In the quiet, secrets hum,
Echoes of a distant drum.
Whispers flutter like the leaves,
In this stillness, the heart believes.

Through the void, the silence sings,
Softest notes, the joy it brings.
Moments pause, the world stands still,
In the quiet, time can thrill.

Listen close, the silence speaks,
Hidden truths in gentle peaks.
Every heartbeat, a soft tune,
Filling spaces with the moon.

In the depths of calm embrace,
Find the beauty in this place.
In the silence, souls connect,
Whispered dreams we won't forget.

Shadows of Serene Sorrow

In twilight's hush, shadows fall,
Silent whispers gently call.
A heart encased in quiet pain,
Drifting softly, like a rain.

Starlit skies, a solemn glow,
Memories wrapped in tangled woe.
Each moment lingers, sweet yet bare,
Caught in the stillness of despair.

Through the night, the shadows dance,
Lost in thoughts of fleeting chance.
Yet in sorrow, beauty lies,
A soft sigh beneath the skies.

Hope will bloom, though shadows play,
In the dusk, a brighter day.
From sorrow's depths, new dreams arise,
To chase the clouds from tear-streaked eyes.

Daisies of Delightful Memories

In fields where laughter used to sway,
Daisies bright chase clouds away.
Each petal holds a tale untold,
A dance of joy amid the gold.

Sun-kissed days of childhood sun,
Every moment, just begun.
Fleeting echoes in the breeze,
Time stands still, sweet memories tease.

With every bloom, a heart's delight,
Childhood whispers in the night.
Gentle breezes stir the past,
Memories cherished, meant to last.

In the garden of our mind,
Beauty found, love intertwined.
Daisies bloom, forever here,
In delight, we hold them dear.

The Budding of Inner Realms

In whispered thoughts, new worlds awake,
A journey starts, a path we take.
Within the soul, a garden grows,
Unknown depths where vision flows.

Petals soft, unfurling grace,
A dance of light in sacred space.
Each bud holds promise, vibrant, pure,
In inner realms, we find our cure.

Beneath the surface, dreams take flight,
Igniting sparks in endless night.
A realm of wonder, vast and wide,
Where hope and courage shall abide.

With every breath, a new refrain,
In budding realms, we break the chain.
A tapestry of quests begun,
In our hearts, we'll always run.

A Labyrinth of Love's Complexity

In winding paths of love's embrace,
We lose ourselves, then find our place.
Each twist and turn, a tale unfolds,
A labyrinth where hearts are bold.

Through shadowed halls of joy and fear,
We seek the light, drawing near.
In every corner, secrets lie,
In tangled thoughts, we learn to fly.

But love is not a straightened line,
In depth and breadth, the stars align.
With every heartbeat, we explore,
The labyrinth opens another door.

Together we weave, in dance or strife,
The complex beauty of our life.
Within this maze, we learn to be,
Two souls entwined, in harmony.

The Language of Sighs

Whispers linger in the air,
Weight of words left unsaid,
Silent stories deep within,
Echoes of the heart's dread.

In the stillness, feelings brew,
Tender pleas without a sound,
Glimmers of hope, shadows too,
In between, the lost are found.

Eyes that speak, hearts that ache,
Moments pass, yet time stands still,
With every sigh, a choice we make,
To love, to lose, to feel, to heal.

Through the night, the stars will guide,
Each sigh a step, a gentle plea,
In the dance where shadows hide,
A language only hearts can see.

Corals of Tenderness

Ocean deep, a world so bright,
Corals dance with every wave,
Colors blend, a pure delight,
Nature's hues, so bold and brave.

Gentle currents whisper tales,
Of love that ebbs and flows like tide,
In this realm where heart prevails,
Tenderness will be our guide.

Beneath the surface, secrets lie,
Wonders that the eye can't find,
In the depths where hopes can fly,
Hearts entwined, forever bind.

Let us dive into this bliss,
In the depths where dreams hold fast,
Finding peace in every kiss,
In the ocean, shadows past.

Seasons of the Heart

Spring awakens with a kiss,
Blossoms bloom, a tender start,
Promises wrapped within a wish,
Dance of love within the heart.

Summer's warmth ignites the flame,
Laughter echoes, skies are bright,
Every joy, we share the same,
Holding close through day and night.

Autumn descends, leaves turn gold,
Whispers of a love grown old,
In the chill, our hands will clasp,
Through the change, we'll ever last.

Winter's breath brings quiet peace,
In the silence, love will grow,
As seasons shift, our hearts release,
In every ebb, we both will know.

In the Shade of Solitude

Beneath the tree, I find my bliss,
Shadows dance, a soothing balm,
In this stillness, thoughts amiss,
    Nature weaves a quiet calm.

Whispers float upon the breeze,
A gentle touch, a soft embrace,
Within these thoughts, I find my peace,
Time drifts slow, a tranquil space.

Alone, yet never truly lost,
In solitude, I learn to see,
The beauty found in silence tossed,
    Finding strength in quiet glee.

Moments linger, shadows pass,
In the shade, my spirit flies,
Embracing truth, like blades of grass,
In solitude, my heart complies.

The Crescendo of Care

In shadows soft, we gather near,
With whispered hopes, we shed the fear.
A gentle touch, a loving hand,
Together strong, we take a stand.

Through trials faced, we share the weight,
In unity, we weave our fate.
Each act of love, a note that soars,
Creating peace, opening doors.

With every heartbeat, pulses rise,
Empathy shines through tearful eyes.
In moments shared, we find our way,
A melody of hope at play.

The crescendo builds, we lift our song,
In harmony, where we belong.
Through care and warmth, we intertwine,
A symphony of hearts divine.

Currents of Compassion

Beneath the surface, the waters flow,
Invisible threads that connect us so.
With every wave, our kindness spreads,
In currents deep where love embeds.

In gentle tides, we find our place,
Embracing all in warm embrace.
Each ripple made by what we share,
A bond that blooms, a world laid bare.

The ocean vast, it knows our names,
In whispered breezes, it plays our games.
With tides of hope that lift and sway,
We navigate through night and day.

Together we drift on this vast sea,
Compassionate hearts, wild and free.
In rhythms of life, we intertwine,
Forever flowing, yours and mine.

A Symphony of Solitude

In quiet chambers where silence sings,
The echoes dance on fragile wings.
Alone, yet safe within my mind,
A world of dreams I long to find.

Each star above, a note so bright,
Guides me through the velvet night.
In solitude, I learn to see,
The beauty born from being free.

Moments linger, like soft refrain,
In breathless hush, I shed my pain.
The heart unfolds, a gentle sigh,
In silence deep, my spirit flies.

This symphony plays a soothing tune,
Awakening thoughts, like a silver moon.
In stillness found, I find my song,
A melody of where I belong.

The Pulse of the Past

In distant echoes, memories tell,
Of moments lived, where shadows dwell.
Each heartbeat marks a timeless trace,
A journey drawn, a steadfast grace.

Through autumn leaves and winter's chill,
The past remains, a constant thrill.
In laughter shared and tears we shed,
The tapestry of life is spread.

Like rivers flowing, time won't cease,
It carries whispers born of peace.
Through every trial, we find our way,
The pulse of love will always stay.

With every step, we homage pay,
To those who shaped our yesterday.
In reverence, we hold the fast,
For in our hearts, beats the past.

Cascading Tears

In silence, droplets fall,
Each one tells a tale,
Washing sorrow, bringing peace,
Like whispers on a trail.

Memories softly drift,
In shadows of the night,
A river deep within,
Holding dreams, taking flight.

Stars above seem to weep,
Mirroring our fears,
Yet through the darkest storms,
Hope glimmers through the tears.

Embrace the cleansing rain,
Let it flow and free,
Cascading tears will shape
The heart's quiet decree.

The Symphony of Sensation

Whispers in the breeze,
Softly brush my skin,
Each note a tender touch,
    Awakening within.

Colors dance around me,
In vibrant, bold parade,
A canvas filled with life,
In hues that never fade.

The taste of sunlit moments,
A sweetness on the tongue,
    Each flavor intertwines,
A song forever sung.

In rhythm, hearts will beat,
To nature's timeless song,
As the symphony of life,
Plays on, where we belong.

Lanterns of Light and Lament

In the stillness of the night,
Lanterns softly glow,
Guiding souls through shadows,
Where whispered sorrows flow.

Each flicker holds a story,
Of loss and love entwined,
In the dance of memories,
Our hopes are redefined.

With every gentle flame,
A heartache finds its voice,
Illuminating pathways,
In the darkness, we rejoice.

Together in the silence,
We find the strength to dream,
For lanterns of light and lament,
Reveal life's fragile gleam.

Embers of Affection

In the hearth of our hearts,
Embers flicker bright,
Warming the cool evenings,
In love's tender light.

Through seasons of the soul,
We gather, side by side,
With laughter like the flame,
In which we take our pride.

When storms may come to call,
We'll kindle every spark,
For in the darkest hours,
Our love shall leave its mark.

In ashes, seeds are sown,
From which new dreams arise,
Embers of affection
Will blaze across the skies.

The Orchard of Longing

In the orchard, whispers weave,
Branches sway with tales believed.
Fruits of dreams hang on each tree,
Yearning hearts seek to be free.

Petals fall like fleeting sighs,
Rippling thoughts beneath the skies.
Shadows blend in twilight's glow,
Where lost desires gently flow.

A breeze carries soft regrets,
Among the boughs, hope offsets.
Roots entwine in silent prayer,
For love that lingers in the air.

Underneath the moon's embrace,
Every shadow knows the place.
In this orchard, hearts shall mend,
With every breeze, the yearnings blend.

When Shadows Dance

When shadows dance on city streets,
Echoes hide in hurried beats.
Underneath the silver glow,
Secrets weave in soft, slow flow.

Figures shift in darkened lanes,
Life unfolds in silent chains.
Every corner, every glance,
Holds a wistful, fleeting chance.

Beneath the stars, a stage is set,
Waltzing dreams that we forget.
As night whispers its sweet song,
Lost within where we belong.

With every turn, a truth revealed,
In shadows' grasp, our fate concealed.
Through the dance, we'll find our way,
In night's embrace, come what may.

Essence of the Unsaid

In the silence, feelings bloom,
Words unspoken fill the room.
Eyes converse in lingering gaze,
Depth of love in quiet ways.

Moments drift on whispering air,
Silent vows, in heart laid bare.
Promises made without a sound,
In the stillness, love is found.

Every glance, a tale untold,
In the hush, emotions bold.
Steps we take in soft retreat,
Echoes of a heartbeat's beat.

In shadows where the secrets lie,
We find the truth that binds the shy.
Essence wrapped in tender thread,
In the layers of words unsaid.

Meadows of Memory

In meadows green, where echoes play,
Time unwinds in bright array.
Dancing flowers, scents so sweet,
Whispers of the past repeat.

Footsteps linger on the path,
Fleeting moments, gentle wrath.
Every blade a tale of yore,
In the silence, we explore.

Here, the sun paints golden dreams,
Through the leaves, the sunlight gleams.
With laughter held in every breeze,
Memories bloom like autumn trees.

As twilight casts its soft embrace,
Time stands still in this safe space.
In the meadows, hearts unite,
Finding solace in the night.

Dewdrops of Delight

Glistening on the morning grass,
Nature's jewels, a gentle class.
They catch the light, a moment's grace,
Whispering joy in this tranquil space.

Beneath the blooms, soft colors gleam,
Each dewdrop holds a waking dream.
A fleeting touch from the dawn's embrace,
Waking hearts in a calm place.

With every step, they play and dance,
Inviting souls to take a chance.
In the quiet, pure and bright,
We find our peace in dewdrops' light.

As they fade with the sun's warm rise,
We carry their spark, our sweet surprise.
In simple things, we find our might,
In dewdrops' world, we find delight.

The Serene Chorus

In whispering winds, a soft refrain,
Nature sings of sun and rain.
With every rustle, a harmony flows,
Life's gentle tune, as the river goes.

The leaves join in, a soothing sound,
A symphony where peace is found.
Birds in flight, a serenade sweet,
The world calms in this rhythmic beat.

Mountains echo, valleys reply,
Under the vast and endless sky.
Every moment, an eternal song,
In the chorus of life, we all belong.

Let us pause and hear the call,
In nature's arms, we rise or fall.
For in this melody, we find our way,
The serene chorus guides our day.

Treasures of Tranquility

Hidden gems in silent streams,
Whispers of peace, soft as dreams.
Among the trees, solace we find,
A gentle balm for the weary mind.

Each breath we take, a soft caress,
In nature's arms, we find our rest.
With every rustle, a promise clear,
Treasures of tranquility near.

A world untouched by the rush of life,
Free from chaos, free from strife.
Here, the heart learns to be still,
In this haven, we find our will.

Let us gather these treasures rare,
Moments of calm, beyond compare.
In the quiet, we truly see,
The treasures of tranquility.

Lanterns of Lost Dreams

Flickering lights in the depth of night,
Guiding our souls to what feels right.
Each lantern glows with a tale untold,
Echoes of wishes, both shy and bold.

Once brighter flames, now flickering low,
Memories linger, like wind's gentle blow.
Yet in their glow, a hope reclaims,
Lanterns of lost dreams still have names.

With every spark, a path unfolds,
Stories of love, of courage, of old.
In their warmth, we find our way,
Through shadows deep to the light of day.

So let us light these lanterns bright,
To honor dreams that took their flight.
In the heart's embrace, we shall glean,
The beauty found in what once had been.

Flickers of Hope

In the darkness, a glimmer shines,
A whisper of dreams, a spark divine.
Through shadows deep, it finds a way,
Guiding lost souls to a brighter day.

With every step, the flame may grow,
Fuelled by belief, it starts to flow.
Hearts once heavy, now lift and soar,
Embracing the light, forevermore.

When storms arise and winds grow fierce,
The flickers dance, our fears it pierce.
Together we stand, hand in hand,
With flickers of hope, we make our stand.

So let us cherish each tiny flame,
For in our hearts, they are not the same.
A beacon of love, a sign to cope,
In every flicker, we find our hope.

Radial Echoes

In whispers soft, the echoes ring,
Reverberating tales from everything.
Across the shores, the stories flow,
Bringing distant dreams, a warm glow.

Patterns spiral, like leaves in dance,
Catch the rhythm, seize the chance.
From every voice, a different hue,
Radial echoes, alive and true.

In silent nights, the chorus hums,
A melody of where we come from.
In every heart, a beat we share,
Radial echoes fill the air.

Together as one, we find our grace,
In every moment, a sacred space.
Let echoes guide our way ahead,
With every tone, our spirits fed.

Hues of Heartache

Crimson shades of sorrow's plight,
Brush strokes bleed through endless night.
Whispers of pain, in colors deep,
Hues of heartache, secrets we keep.

The twilight speaks in shades of gray,
Memories linger, colors sway.
Each tear a drop, a story paved,
In hues of heartache, love is braved.

Yet in the dark, a glimmer glows,
Painting the night with tender prose.
A canvas rich with what we've learned,
In hues of heartache, hearts discerned.

Through colors dark, we find our way,
Creating beauty in disarray.
For every sorrow, a lesson drawn,
In hues of heartache, we carry on.

The Colors of Care

Softest greens of gentle hand,
Brush against our hearts, they stand.
In every glance, a silent vow,
The colors of care, here and now.

Golden rays of warmth and light,
Wrap around us, shining bright.
Through trials faced, we find our grace,
In the colors of care, we find our place.

Deepest blues of tranquil thought,
Pause in moments, lessons taught.
In every heartbeat, love we share,
Echoing softly, the colors of care.

Let hues unite as bridges soar,
Each shade of kindness opens doors.
Together we weave a tapestry rare,
In every thread, the colors of care.

The Forest of Yearning

In the woods where shadows play,
The whispering leaves call my name.
Footsteps trace a winding way,
Hearts entwined in nature's game.

A canopy of dreams above,
Every branch a tale untold.
Softly wrapped in arms of love,
As twilight starts to turn to gold.

Roots entwined beneath the ground,
Pulse of life in every breath.
In this silence, hope is found,
Echoes dance beyond death.

In the forest, memories bloom,
With every turn, a path anew.
Yearning for the light from gloom,
Guided by the stars' soft hue.

Ripples of Remembrance

In the stillness of the night,
Whispers linger on the breeze.
Memories shimmer, pure and bright,
Carried softly through the trees.

Each wave a story from the past,
A gentle touch upon my soul.
Rippling echoes, unsurpassed,
Waves of time that make me whole.

Through the waters, shadows glide,
Flashes of a cherished face.
Ripples pulling me inside,
To dance again in time and space.

In the depths of a quiet stream,
I find the strength to carry on.
Ripples whisper, gently beam,
In remembrance, I am not gone.

Starlit Longings

Underneath the vast night sky,
Stars are dreams that gleam and soar.
Wishes carried high and spry,
Unraveled truths we can't ignore.

Each twinkling light, a hope in flight,
Guiding hearts through dark and doubt.
In this quiet, perfect night,
Starlit longings burst about.

Constellations map our fate,
Threads of silver, gold, and blue.
In their glow, we contemplate,
What is old and what is new.

Between the worlds of sleep and dream,
We chase the shadows, faint yet near.
Starlit longings softly gleam,
Whispering truths we long to hear.

The Canvas of Joy

With every brush, a story's spun,
Colors dance on a blank white page.
Laughter echoes, joy begun,
Hearts unleashed from their cage.

Strokes of red, a vibrant hue,
Yellow sunbeams bright and bold.
Shades of green, a world anew,
In this canvas, we feel gold.

Each moment captured, held so tight,
A masterpiece of love and grace.
Through the day, into the night,
Joy's warm essence we embrace.

The canvas calls for every heart,
To paint their dreams in colors free.
With every splash, a brand new start,
In this joy, we long to be.

Blossoms in the Mind

Petals dance on whispered breeze,
Colors blend with gentle ease,
Thoughts take flight on fragrant air,
Dreams awaken, free from care.

In the garden of the heart,
Each bloom a fragile work of art,
Sculpting moments, soft and bright,
Guiding shadows into light.

Memory's light, a tender shade,
In the quiet, joy is made,
Blossoms burst with vibrant hue,
In the mind, they feel so true.

As the seasons softly change,
Every thought begins to range,
Through the fields of what we seek,
Finding beauty in the meek.

The Seedlings of Sentiment

In the soil of tender care,
Hope takes root, meets gentle air,
Each seed a wish, a longing deep,
Planted where the heart can weep.

Nurtured by the sun's embrace,
Time will shape their destined place,
Fragile dreams begin to rise,
Reaching up to paint the skies.

When the storms come, strong and wild,
Still they grow, each wayward child,
Through the trials, they will stay,
Blooming bright along the way.

In the garden of the soul,
Every feeling finds its role,
Connections bloom, both near and far,
Guiding hearts, like shining stars.

Forests of Forgotten Dreams

In shadows deep, where echoes sleep,
The whispers of the past we keep,
Branches twist in tangled thought,
Wandering paths that time forgot.

Leaves that shimmer, soft and green,
Hiding tales that once had been,
Within the grove, the silence hums,
A melody of what becomes.

Ancient roots hold stories tight,
Guiding seekers through the night,
Lost in tales that twist and turn,
In the heart, a fire burns.

Every step draws forth a sigh,
Chasing dreams that learn to fly,
In the forest, wild and vast,
Ember sparks of present, past.

Tides of Turbulent Thoughts

Waves crash hard against the shore,
Rising high, then sinking more,
Thoughts collide in restless swell,
Drowning deep, we rise and fell.

Currents pull, a strong embrace,
Rushing thoughts, a wild race,
Caught between the deep and wide,
In this sea, we must abide.

Fleeting moments, sharp and clear,
Whispers tugging, drawing near,
Tides will shift with every breath,
Bringing life, or thoughts of death.

Yet in storms, there's peace to find,
In the chaos, calmness twined,
Ride the waves, let sorrows part,
In the ocean, heal the heart.

The Thicket of Untamed Affections

In the thicket where shadows play,
Roots intertwine, lost night and day.
Hearts collide like branches high,
Whispers of love, beneath the sky.

Thorns may prick, but blooms remain,
Roses grow amidst the pain.
Each petal soft, a story told,
Of daring hearts, both brave and bold.

Here, in wild, emotions swirl,
A secret dance, a hidden world.
With every sigh, the thicket breathes,
In tangled dreams, the heart believes.

Through the maze, we chase the light,
In untamed affections, we take flight.
Barefoot souls on a path unknown,
In thickets deep, our love has grown.

Hedges of Hopefulness

In hedges green, where dreams take flight,
Hope blooms softly, a guiding light.
Each leaf whispers tales of trust,
In the embrace of love, we must.

Bound by blooms that reach the sun,
Together we walk, our journey begun.
In the shelter of each gentle fold,
Our hopes flourish, brave and bold.

Every thorn guards a tender heart,
In hedges wild, we play our part.
As seasons change, we stand our ground,
In hopefulness, our strength is found.

With every dawn, new visions rise,
Through leafy paths, we seek the skies.
By the hedges, hand in hand we roam,
In the warmth of hope, we find our home.

Garden of Heartstrings

In the garden where heartstrings glow,
Every petal sways to and fro.
Colors burst in vibrant hues,
Whispers of love in morning dews.

Beneath the boughs, secrets lie,
Songs of passion, a gentle sigh.
With every bloom, a promise made,
In this garden, we won't fade.

Roots entwined, we share the earth,
In this space, we find our worth.
Every glance, a tender spark,
In the garden, we leave our mark.

As twilight falls, the stars align,
In the quiet, our souls entwine.
With every heartbeat, life springs new,
In this garden, I cherish you.

Whispers in the Wind

In the night, the winds confess,
Soft whirls carry our tenderness.
Through the trees, our secrets glide,
In whispered dreams, where we confide.

The breeze wraps round, a gentle touch,
In every sigh, I feel so much.
Carried far on currents free,
Whispers speak of you and me.

As leaves dance with the fading light,
Echoes of love fill the night.
With every gust, our hopes align,
In whispers sweet, our hearts entwine.

Through valleys deep, and mountains high,
The wind shall tell of our goodbye.
Yet in every breath, remains a trace,
Of whispered love, a warm embrace.

Horizons of Hopes Unspoken

In the silence, dreams take flight,
Beyond the shadows, out of sight.
Whispers of wishes, soft and bright,
A palette of stars, painting the night.

Glistening dawn kisses the sky,
With every heartbeat, hopes will rise.
Of paths unseen, we dare to try,
As laughter mingles with distant sighs.

Mountains echo with unvoiced sound,
In valleys deep, our spirits found.
Through heavy clouds, we walk around,
In the stillness, truths abound.

Life's canvas stretches, wide and free,
From every heart, we seek to see.
Painting horizons, endlessly,
With colors of hope, eternally.

The Pathways of Vulnerability

In open fields where shadows meet,
The heart's soft whispers find their beat.
With every step, the rawness grows,
In tender moments, grace bestows.

Promises linger in the air,
An earnest gaze, a knowing stare.
In fragile states, we learn to stand,
Hand in hand, we share our land.

Through cracks and scars, the light will seep,
In letting go, our spirits leap.
We stumble, rise, and find our way,
In vulnerability, we choose to stay.

Each pathway bends, yet we walk bold,
In stories shared, our truth unfolds.
Embracing flaws, we learn to sway,
In the dance of life, we find our play.

Soliloquy of Serenity

In stillness, whispers softly flow,
A gentle breeze begins to show.
The heart converses with the night,
In solitude, we find our light.

Beneath the stars, our thoughts align,
In quiet moments, hearts entwine.
Each breath a note in nature's song,
In peace we linger, where we belong.

Reflections in a crystal stream,
Unravel time, we find our dream.
Through waves of calm, we sail away,
In serenity, we choose to stay.

From mountains high to valleys low,
In every heartbeat, love can grow.
With open arms, we greet the dawn,
In the harmony of now, we're drawn.

Waves of Wonder

Across the sea, where dreams collide,
In every crest, the hopes abide.
With salt and spray, our spirits rise,
In every wave, a new surprise.

The moonlight dances on the tide,
With echoes of the world beside.
From shore to shore, we chase the thrill,
In nature's arms, we find our will.

With every crash, the heart beats free,
In whispers of the deep blue sea.
The universe in motion sways,
In waves of wonder, lost in gaze.

Beneath the stars, the magic flows,
As tides reveal what nature knows.
In waves of wonder, hearts unite,
In the ocean's embrace, pure delight.

Melodies in the Mist

Whispers dance on the breeze,
Soft notes drift through the trees.
Morning dew on petals gleams,
Nature sings in gentle dreams.

Clouds wrap the world in hush,
As shadows and light gently blush.
In the fog, the heart can roam,
Finding solace, feeling home.

Each tone a story to tell,
Woven in the magic's spell.
Melodies in the mist appear,
A symphony for hearts to hear.

Nature's voice, a tender guide,
In the silence, dreams abide.
We listen close, we breathe it in,
In melodies, our souls begin.

Labors of Love

Hands toil, hearts entwined,
In each task, our hopes aligned.
Sweat and joy, a grand embrace,
In honest efforts, we find grace.

Brick by brick, we build our dreams,
Flowing like the purest streams.
Through the struggles, bonds grow tight,
In labors of love, our spirits ignite.

Every challenge faced with pride,
Side by side, we shall abide.
With every dawn, we rise anew,
In labors of love, our truth rings true.

Harvest reaped from fields we sowed,
Pathways shaped from the road we strode.
Together we stand, hand in hand,
In life's tapestry, we make our stand.

The Stillness Between

In quietude, a moment holds,
Secrets whispered, life unfolds.
The breath between each word we speak,
A sanctuary for the meek.

In silence, thoughts begin to flow,
Like rivers deep beneath the snow.
Space where clarity can glean,
In the stillness, we find the serene.

The pause before the storm of sound,
A gentle whisper all around.
In the gaps, life draws its breath,
A timeless dance with life and death.

Embrace the calm, let worries cease,
In the stillness, find your peace.
For in those moments, hearts align,
In the stillness, love will shine.

Flavors of Faith

In every heart, a taste resides,
A blend of hopes that never hides.
Spices of belief, sweet and bold,
In flavors of faith, stories unfold.

Savor the warmth, the joy it brings,
In simple acts, the laughter sings.
Through trials faced, we stir the pot,
In flavors of faith, love is sought.

A pinch of trust, a dash of prayer,
Collective dreams fill the air.
In shared moments, we all partake,
Each flavor savored, never fake.

From bitter to sweet, the journey's wide,
In every taste, let hope abide.
A feast of faith, let spirits soar,
In flavors of faith, we long for more.

The Hidden Marshlands of the Spirit

In the whispers of the reeds, they hide,
Secrets murmur, where dreams abide.
Reflections dance on waters still,
Echoes of past, a whispering thrill.

Shadows flicker in twilight's grace,
Each footstep leads to a sacred place.
Fog embraces the wandering soul,
In the marshlands, the heart feels whole.

Nature's breath, a calming song,
In hidden realms where we belong.
A tapestry woven of dusk and dawn,
In these marshlands, we are reborn.

Ferns of Fleeting Moments

Amidst the forest, soft and green,
Ferns unfurl in a quiet scene.
Each moment like a drop of dew,
Glistening bright, ever so new.

Time dances lightly on fragile fronds,
In a world where eternity responds.
A fleeting breath, a whispered sigh,
Beneath the boughs, where memories lie.

Glimmers of life in tangled lace,
Chasing shadows in nature's embrace.
For every heartbeat, a tale unfolds,
In the ferns, the untold beholds.

The Mosaic of Yearning

Shattered pieces of dreams align,
A mosaic formed from hearts that pine.
Colors blend in a tempest's flight,
Yearning whispers in the still of night.

Touched by shadows, kissed by light,
Each fragment tells of love's sweet plight.
The patterns swirl in a cosmic dance,
In every glance, a soulful chance.

Echoes linger in the silent air,
Each yearning heart laid bare,
In the tapestry rich with fate,
The mosaic sings of love's estate.

Brambles of Bittersweet Truths

In corridors where shadows grow,
Brambles twist, bearing tales of woe.
Each thorn a reminder of what was lost,
Bittersweet truths come at a cost.

Memories trapped in tangled vines,
Each moment's echo softly shines.
Through the thicket of love and pain,
We find our way, though it leaves a stain.

Yet in the struggle, there's beauty found,
In the brambles, dreams are unbound.
Through the thorns, we carve our path,
Bittersweet truths, love's aftermath.

Colorful Storms Within

Whispers dance in the night air,
Colors clash without a care.
Thunder rumbles, skies ignite,
A kaleidoscope of pure delight.

Lightning strikes, a vivid flash,
A tempest born from spirits' clash.
Deep within, the storms do roar,
Yet, beauty waits on every shore.

Truths collide in vibrant hue,
Beneath the chaos, dreams break through.
In the heart where storms reside,
A swirling palette, joy's guide.

Let the colors reign and swirl,
Unraveling the hidden pearl.
For in each tempest lies a pearl,
A radiant dance, a life unfurled.

Petals of Reflection

In gardens where soft whispers bloom,
Petals flutter, dismantling gloom.
Mirrored thoughts in morning's light,
Reflecting dreams, taking flight.

Each bloom cradles a silent wish,
In the gentle sway, hearts can bliss.
Colors deepen, shadows blend,
As nature's beauty knows no end.

Rustling leaves lend an ear,
To secrets of the life held dear.
In petals soft, wisdom hides,
Awakening hope, the heart abides.

A dance of moments, fleeting, rare,
In every petal, love lays bare.
With each reflection, grow and learn,
In life's sweet garden, brightly turn.

Harvest of Dreams

Golden fields beneath the sun,
Where every heart's desire is spun.
In every grain, a story sown,
A journey shared, never alone.

From dusk till dawn, we toil and weave,
Collecting hopes, learning to believe.
With every seed, a promise made,
In rich soil, our dreams cascade.

The bounteous yield, so bright and bold,
A tapestry of futures told.
With open hands, we gather near,
The harvest sweet, our path is clear.

In gratitude, we stand as one,
Celebrating what we've begun.
For in this bounty, dreams align,
A shared embrace, where love will shine.

Reflections in the Mirror

Glimmers dance where thoughts collide,
In every crack, our truths abide.
Faces change, yet spirits stay,
In mirrors' gaze, we find our way.

Each glance reveals the stories told,
Of laughter bright and moments bold.
In silenced whispers, shadows play,
Reflecting back another day.

Emotions swirl, a hidden stream,
Where dreams and worries intertwine and teem.
With every touch, the glass reveals,
The heart's own pulse, its quiet appeals.

So let us pause, and take a glance,
At journeys lived within life's dance.
For in the mirror, we are found,
In reflections deep, our souls unbound.

Milton Keynes UK
Ingram Content Group UK Ltd.
UKHW020151291024
450401UK00007B/112